BUTTERFLIES
of Australia

Paul Zborowski

First published in 2022 by Reed New Holland Publishers
Sydney

Level 1, 178 Fox Valley Road, Wahroonga, NSW 2076, Australia

newhollandpublishers.com

A record of this book is held at the National Library of Australia.

ISBN 978 1 92554 694 1

Managing Director: Fiona Schultz
Publisher and Project Editor: Simon Papps
Designer: Andrew Davies
Production Director: Arlene Gippert
Printed in China

10 9 8 7 6 5 4 3 2

Keep up with New Holland Publishers:
 NewHollandPublishers and ReedNewHolland
 @newhollandpublishers

Front cover: Green-spotted Triangle, *Graphium agamemnon*
Back cover: Blue Argus, *Junonia orithya*
Page 1: Australian Admiral, *Vanessa itea*

CONTENTS

Tailed Emperor, *Charaxes sempronius*.

Introduction

3

The Butterflies

INTRODUCTION

What is a Butterfly

Butterflies and moths belong to the insect order Lepidoptera. Orders are higher-level classification groups, like all beetles (Coleoptera), or all flies (Diptera). The order name is made up of the Greek words lepis, meaning 'scale', and pteron, meaning 'wing'. This defines all butterflies and moths, as their bodies and wings are covered in overlapping scales. Even what look like hairs, especially in moths, are just denser and finer scales. The other characteristic feature is the mouthparts, which are tubular, long, and coiled in butterflies and most moths. This is called a proboscis, or tongue, and is inserted into flowers to feed on sugars, which power the short lives of the flying adults. This proboscis can be as long as the body when fully straightened, and this allows feeding and drinking from deep flowers. Antennae are thickened at the ends, in what is known as a club. There are currently 398 species of butterflies recognised on the Australian mainland and Tasmania. That number climbs to 416 when outlying islands and migrant species are included.

The Butterfly or Moth question

The order Lepidoptera has more than 10,800 named species in 93 families in Australia alone. The butterflies are simply 6 families containing about 400 species of day-flying 'moths' with a suite of characters that makes them, mostly, distinct. They have the

Close up of the wing of a Ulysses Swallowtail showing the scales.

thickened, clubbed antennae; all except the Regent Skipper lack velcro-like hooks joining the wings in flight, which moths use to beat their wings in unison; they tend to perch with their wings upright; and there are minor differences in the pupa. There are very colourful moths, some that fly by day, and even a few with thickened antennae, but no true moths have all the butterfly characters in combination.

Evolution

The earliest known moths are tiny, have no proboscis, and date back to around 300 million years ago. They were associated with pre-flowering plant groups. The current butterfly families probably originated about 75 million years ago, at a time when flowering

Who said moths are not as colourful as butterflies? This is the Queensland Day Moth, *Alcides metaurus*.

plants were proliferating. The oldest known fossil of these delicate organisms is 40 million years old, and that species was already very much like modern butterflies.

Life cycle

Butterflies belong to the insect groups which undergo full metamorphosis and have a sequence consisting of egg, caterpillar, pupa and adult. Eggs are commonly laid on the foodplant leaves. They are usually glued under the leaf to protect them from the weather and some predators. Both the antennae and the 'feet', the tarsi of the adults, have chemoreceptors to taste if the plant is the right one to eat. Larger guide books – such as *A Field Guide to*

Butterflies of Australia: Their Life Histories and Larval Food Plants
by Garry Sankowsky and Geoff Walker (Reed New Holland, 2020)
– list the food plants used by different species. This is very useful
knowledge if you want to attract butterflies to your garden, and help
their survival. When the caterpillars hatch they start a relentless
feeding binge. In a few weeks their mass can increase 1,000-fold,
helped by shedding their 'skin', the exoskeleton, five or six times.
Each stage is called an instar. Caterpillars of butterflies and moths
have the insect-usual three pairs of legs on the thorax. But they also
have four pairs of short 'prolegs' on segments of their abdomen,
which help them to cling to leaves.

Caterpillar of the Ambrax Swallowtail, *Papilio ambrax*, shedding its 'skin', or exoskeleton,
to reveal a new larger one to grow into.

The majority of butterfly larvae are leaf feeders, but a few, especially among the Blues (Lycaenidae), the caterpillar may live with ants, and in a few species they eat the ant larvae. All the ant-associated Lyceanid larvae give the ants a sweet secretion known as honeydew from nectary glands on the abdomen. In return, the ants help to protect the exposed caterpillars.

Cairns Birdwing butterfly larvae just hatched.

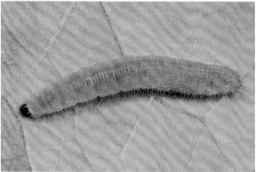

Cabbage White butterfly showing typical life-cycle sequence, from sculpted egg to

caterpillar, to chrysalis or pupa, and adults mating to make more eggs.

Leafwing, *Doleschallia bisaltide*, emerging from its chrysalis.

When the last instar is fully grown, the caterpillar attaches itself with silk to a structure such as a twig, and changes into the pupa, also known as the chrysalis. Each family has fairly characteristic variations regarding the shape and attachment method of the pupa. After some days or weeks, the butterfly emerges from this case, expands its wet crinkled wings, and flies away looking for a mate. Some pupae wait for right conditions for months, and even for a year or more.

Habits

Adult butterflies have colour vision and often very showy wings. Therefore some have quite elaborate mid-air courtship dances before mating choices are made. Males are often territorial and choose open places to gather, such as grassy hilltops, where they are most visible. This is known as 'hilltopping' and presents a good opportunity for butterfly observers. Females visit these areas briefly to mate.

Many moths store enough food from the caterpillar stage to not need to feed at all as adults. Butterfly adults do feed, but mainly to obtain sugars from flowers for flight energy. The proteins for egg making are carried over from the caterpillar. Some butterflies, especially males, also sometimes feed from riverbanks, puddles and other damp patches, which have available sodium. They transfer this

Male Orange Palm Dart, *Cephrenes trichopepla* feeding on minerals found in a bird dropping.

Courtship display, and mating, in the Orchard Swallowtail, *Papilio aegeus*, with the male above the female.

to the females while mating, which aids in egg production.

Other sources of minerals, such as dung, bird droppings and rotting fruit, are also sometimes visited. Most adults live for two to three weeks, although some can live for several months with periods of inactivity.

About three-quarters of our butterfly species can be found in the tropical regions, especially coastal Qld. Some of these extend to southern climes, but species numbers drop with colder and drier climates. Only about 90 species are recorded (not continuously) from the interior, and none live above about 1,600m in altitude. Some butterflies do what is called 'aggregating'. This is a period of slowed down metabolism, a dormancy, to survive until a dry or cold season is over, and their foodplants again green up. Such species are very long lived as adults, often for a year or more.

Classification

As mentioned, butterflies occupy just a small corner of the order Lepidoptera, which has 30 groups of families, known as superfamilies. Butterflies represent two of these in Australia. A third small, often night-flying, group of butterflies is found in South and Central America.

The Hesperoidea has one family, the Hesperiidae, or Skippers, with 121 species of these quick darting small butterflies. They differ by having the antennae inserted wide apart on the head, with a long slowly thickening club ending on a little curved thin segment. They also sometimes sit with the hindwings splayed out flat, and only the forewings held upright. Recent studies of butterfly

15

phylogenomics suggest that this superfamily in fact belongs within the Papilionoidea, along with all other Australian butterflies.

The Papilionoidea has five families. The Papilionidae, mainly large species known as Swallowtails. The Nymphalidae, 81 mainly medium-sized species, with brown colours predominating, known as Nymphs and Browns. The Pieridae are the Whites and Yellows, with 35 medium to small white and yellow species. The Lycaenidae, 142 species of smallish butterflies with blue dominant on their upperside wings, and often other colours on the underside, are known as the Blues. The final family, the Riodinidae, have visual features of the Nymphs and Blues, and are known as Metalmarks, with only one species in Australia.

How to Use This Guide

The pictures in this guide are mainly taken in the field, showing live butterflies doing what they do, and how they do it. This includes the important aspect of how they perch when resting. Most butterflies sit with their wings closed and upright. Hence we only see the underside wing colours and patterns, and a flash of the upperside as the butterfly flies around. Early in the mornings, when they are cold, you can be lucky and find them with open wings in the sun, warming up the flight muscles. Therefore the pictures here reflect the reality of what you will encounter in the field. Most images are of perched feeding butterflies with closed wings. Some show the open wing pose of the warming phase, or both where possible. Some caterpillars are included. They may be easy to spot sometimes, and give one warning of what species may be present in the area,

Red Lacewing, *Cethosia cydippe*.

before spotting the short-lived adult. A few species are shown
from mounted specimens where an 'in the bush' example was not
available. Each species chosen here represents various groups, such
as a particular genus, or common name group. Wingspan sizes are
an average of the range.

Some butterflies use a very broad range of caterpillar foodplants.
Available space in this book means not all plant species are
included, but sources for more detailed works are listed at the end.
Where available, representative caterpillars of various species are
included.

The 'active during' information is an indication of when adults
may be encountered. Caterpillars may have a broader range of
times. Geographically, some pictures of species from Western
Australia and Tasmania have been deliberately chosen, to make sure
that this guide is not east-centric, as often happens in publications.

Species names

Common names generally follow those used in *A Field Guide to Butterflies of Australia: Their Life Histories and Larval Food Plants* by Garry Sankowsky and Geoff Walker (Reed New Holland, 2020). Some scientific names have an extra name in brackets, reflecting a recent name change, and providing the means to search for more information on that species in older publications.

Abbreviations

sp	=	species
Jan, Feb, Mar, etc	=	January, February, March, etc
N, E, S, W	=	north, east, south, west, etc
NE, SW	=	North-east, south-west, etc
ACT	=	Australian Capital Territory
NSW	=	New South Wales
NT	=	Northern Territory
Qld	=	Queensland
SA	=	South Australia
Tas	=	Tasmania
Vic	=	Victoria
WA	=	Western Australia

Wanderer, *Danaus plexippus.*

THE BUTTERFLIES

SKIPPERS –
FAMILY HESPERIIDAE

Fast erratic flyers, settling often, the skippers are 121 Australian species out of 3,500 species worldwide. The head is broader and larger in relation to the rest of the body than in other butterflies, with the antennae wide apart. The body is comparatively short and stout. At rest many hold the hindwings flat and the forewings upright. Some perch with wings flat, or upright when fully warmed up, others perch with wings fully open flat.

Caterpillars are rarely seen as they hide in leaf shelters during the day and feed at night. Pupa are also usually well hidden. Colours are most often browns with cream markings. Several species are very small, with wingspans down to 18mm. Average size for members of this family is about 30–35mm.

Caterpillar of one of the dusk flat skippers, *Chaetocneme* sp.

Regent Skipper *Euschemon rafflesia*

ID: This is the brightest skipper in Australia, with aposematic yellow-red-blue patterns against a black background. There are two very similar subspecies: *E.r. rafflesia* in N NSW and SE Qld coasts; and *E.r. alba* in coastal N Qld.

HABITS: Found mainly in rainforest areas, where the males fly in the morning and at dusk, and gather on more open hilltops near forest. Sometimes attracted to lights during dusk flights. Relatively common in their localised areas. Foodplants include *Tetrasynandra pubescens* and *Wilkiea huegeliana*.

Purple Dusk Flat *Chaetocneme porphyropis*

ID: Large skipper. Only the Banded Red-eye (*C. critomedia*) has similar patterns, but its main colour is dark copper-brown. Found from about Cooktown to Townsville, Qld. Wingspan 56mm.

HABITS: Flies in lowland and tableland rainforests, and active until dusk. Foodplants include laurels in the genera *Neolitsea*, *Cryptocarya* and *Endiandra*.

Eastern Flat *Netrocoryne repanda*

ID: Beautiful deep bronze with cream markings. Two subspecies: *N.r. repanda* from about Rockhampton, Qld, to the Vic border (40mm wingspan); and the smaller *N.r. expansa* in N Qld.

HABITS: rapid flyer in rainforests and open woodland. Males territorial and hilltop in open woodland. By late afternoon they can sometimes be found resting on undersides of leaves, with fully open flat wings. Foodplants include species of *Endiandra*, *Callicoma* and *Eleocarpus*.

Green Awl *Hasora discolora*

ID: Very distinctive, with dark bronze/green upperside and a broad bright yellow band down the centre of the underside hindwing. Found in patches along the Qld coast from Cape York to NSW border.

HABITS: Fast flyer in rainforests and vine thickets. Foodplants are vines in the woody liana genus *Mucuna*.

Narrow-banded Awl *Hasora khoda*

ID: Deep brown with a faint purplish sheen on upperside. Two spots on each upper forewing in female. Found from Sunshine Coast, Qld, to about Bega, coastal NSW. Wingspan 40–45mm.

HABITS: Fast flyer with males forming territories in forest patches. Temperate rainforests and wet sclerophyll areas, where may overwinter as adults in sheltered areas. Main foodplant is the legume *Millettia megasperma*.

Male upperside and underside.

25

Wedge Grass Skipper *Anisynta sphenosema*

ID: Hard to discern from other species of *Anisynta* in the field, but it is the only member of the genus in WA. Found around Perth, parts of S coast, and near Esperance. Wingspan 25mm.

HABITS: Fast daytime flyer in open woodland, near creeks, and in suburban gardens. Active Mar–May, some areas from Dec.

Two-brand Grass Skipper *Anisynta dominula*

ID: Small, chocolate brown, with two (male) or five (female) cream marks on upper forewings. Wingspan 26–28mm. Two subspecies: *A.d. dominula* from N SW to S Vic and E Tas; and *A.d. pria* in NW Tas.

HABITS: This is a hill and mountain species, found from about 600–1,600m altitude in alpine grasslands and open woodlands, where they fly for only a few warm hours each day. Active Jan–Mar. Foodplants are grasses of the genus *Poa*.

Mountain Grass Skipper *Anisynta monticolae*

ID: Similar to *A. dominula* (previous entry), but with the patterns on upperside forewings same shape but larger, and three extra small yellow bars on hindwing. Underwing with more extensive white areas. Found in grassy open woodlands along the Great Divide, at 600–1,300m, from S NSW to E Vic.

HABITS: Flies low, settling in sunny areas. Foodplants are grasses, especially genus *Poa*.

Splendid Ochre *Trapezites symmomus*

ID: There are 18 Australian species in this genus, roughly characterised by square or rectangular cream markings on brown bodies. *T. symmomus* is one of the bolder species with very dark brown wings contrasting with the cream markings. Three subspecies: *T.s. symmomus* from S Qld to Vic border; *T.s. soma* in S Vic; and *T.s. sombra* on the Atherton Tableland, Qld. Wingspan 45mm.

HABITS: Flies rapidly in open woodland, clearings and gardens, were the main foodplant, the sedge *Lomandra longifolia* (Basket Grass), and other *Lomandra* sp are found. Active Jan-Mar.

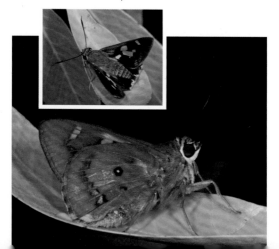

Yellow Ochre *Trapezites luteus*

ID: Similar to some other species in this genus, but differs by underside hindwing being more yellow than fawn/brown, and its single spot there not strongly ringed by black. Three subspecies: *T.l. luteus* near Adelaide, SA; *T.l. glaucus* in Tas; and *T.l. leucon* in patches from SE Qld to Vic. Wingspan 30mm.

HABITS: Flies in open woodlands and grasslands, up to 1,700m altitude in NSW. Foodplants are many species of the mat rush genus *Lomandra*.

T.l. glaucus in Tasmania.

Alpine Sedge Skipper *Oreisplanus munionga*

ID: The striking yellow-black underwing pattern is more useful for ID than the upperside of brown with cream spots. Found only in high ground, from about 1,000–1,600m in Vic and NSW Alps, and subspecies *O.m. larana* in NW Tas. Wingspan 25–30mm.

HABITS: Flies close to low vegetation in open alpine woodland and waterways. Mainly active in Feb. Main foodplant is *Carex appressa*.

Flame Sedge Skipper *Hesperilla idothea*

ID: Genus contains several similar species. This one has just three small spots on the pale brown underside hindwing, others have four or more. Two subspecies: *H.i. idothea* from Brisbane, Qld, through E NSW, most of Vic and in Tas. *H.i. clara* in tiny patch south of Adelaide, SA. Wingspan 38mm.

HABITS: Fast flyer in open woodland and wetter forests and gullies. Foodplants are species of saw-sedge in the genus *Gahnia*.

Inset: *H.i. idothea* in Tasmania.

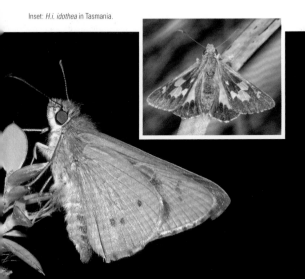

Varied Sedge Skipper *Hesperilla donnysa*

ID: Has five or six small black spots in a line on underside hindwing, compared to three in similar *H. idothea*, and underside colour is more pale brown/grey than orange. Four subspecies: *H.d. donnysa* from SE Qld, E NSW and most of Vic to Adelaide, SA; *H.d. galena* and *H.d. albina* in SW WA; and *H.d. aurantia* in Tas. Wingspan 31–36mm.

HABITS: Fast flyer in open woodlands, heathlands and alpine forests up to 1,500m. Foodplants are species of saw-sedge in the genus *Gahnia*.

H.d. aurantia from Tas.

Spotted Sedge Skipper *Hesperilla ornata*

ID Very similar to the Mountain Sedge Skipper (*H. perornatus*), which is restricted to the Vic and NSW high country. Very bold chocolate on white underside markings. Two subspecies: *H.o. monotherma* in N Qld; and *H.o. ornata* in S Qld, all of NSW coastal and S Vic. Wingspan 30–35mm.

HABITS: Fast flyer in open woodland, heath and creek gullies. Foodplants are sedges in the genera *Gahnia* and *Carex*.

Western Brown Skipper *Motasingha dirphia*

ID: In resting position with closed wings, one larger and one smaller white spot on pale pink-brown hindwing is typical. Not common, found in patches of heath and open woodland in WA between about Geraldton and Esperance. Wingspan 35mm.

HABITS: Very little known, though it has been found to hilltop. Active Oct–Nov. Even the foodplant is still not recorded.

Western Sand Skipper *Antipodia dactyliota*

ID: Very similar to other sand skipper species in other states, but lives only in WA, from about Geraldton to Esperance. Subspecies *A.d. nila* has very restricted range around Carnarvon area. Wingspan 30–35mm.

HABITS: Lives in open woodland and heath, in more sandy country where its foodplants – several species of *Gahnia* saw-sedge – are found. Active Oct–Nov.

Nominate subspecies *A.d. dactyliota*.

Two-spotted Grass Skipper *Pasma tasmanica*

ID: Dark brown upperside with five cream markings on forewings and two tiny spots on hindwings. Pale underside. Found along E NSW, much of Vic and most of Tas. Wingspan 24mm.

HABITS: Flies low in open woodland and forests from coastal areas to 1,200m altitude on the mainland and 900m in Tas. Foodplants are grasses in the *Microlaena* and *Poa* genera.

Barred Skipper *Dispar compacta*

ID: Similar to grass skippers, but differs from most by having either single (in female) or triple (in male) elongate yellow markings on upperside hindwings. Found from SE Qld coast, along NSW coast to E Vic. Wingspan 23mm.

HABITS: Flies low in open woodlands and heaths. Males hilltop. Foodplants include species of *Poa* and *Lomandra* grasses.

Lilac Grass Skipper *Toxidia doubledayi*

ID: Chocolate-brown upperside with three irregular cream markings on forewing, one of which consists of three tiny spots in a line. No markings on hindwing. Found in tropical Qld coast, then SE Qld and along NSW coast to E Vic. Wingspan 26mm.

HABITS: Flies fast in open woodlands and along creeks. Foodplants are grasses in *Oplismenus* and *Microlaena* genera.

Banded Demon *Notocrypta waigensis*

ID: Very dark brown with large bold white band across the forewing on upperside and underside. Wingspan 35–38mm.

HABITS: Rainforests and monsoon forests in N Qld, all the way to tip of Cape York. Active mainly in wet season from Dec–Apr. Adults can feed from deep flowers, with a proboscis longer than the body. Main foodplant is *Alpinia caerulea*.

No-brand Grass Dart *Taractrocera ina*

ID: One of many similar species in the genera *Taractrocera* and *Telicota*. Has a broad, patchy distribution along most of Qld coast, and in NT around Litchfield and even Alice Springs. Small at 22–25mm wingspan.

HABITS: Flies in coastal open woodland, and in open grass plains in the interior. Foodplants are grasses, mainly *Paspalum*, *Panicum*, *Sorghum* and *Cymbopogon* sp.

White-banded Grass Dart *Taractrocera papyria*

ID: Small dart, 20mm wingspan. Two subspecies: *T.p. papyria* in N Qld, E NSW, most of Vic to Adelaide in SA, and E Tas; *T.p. agraulia* in patches of SW WA.

HABITS: Low flying, even perching on the ground sometimes. Active in the east from Oct–May. Foodplants are grasses, including spear grass *Austrostipa*, *Cynodon*, *Imperata* sp and more.

Large Yellow Grass Dart *Taractrocera anisomorpha*

ID: Very similar to the No-brand Grass Dart, and with similar range. Found along most of the Qld coast, and in patches in the NT and Pilbara, WA. Wingspan 24mm.

HABITS: Found in open woodland and inland watercourses. Foodplants are grasses in the *Setaria*, *Eulalia* and *Sorghum* genera.

Walker's Grass Dart *Ocybadistes walkeri*

ID: The grass darts are very small, 20mm wingspans, and very hard to pick apart from other dart species. Three subspecies: *O.w. sothis* along most of E Qld, NSW, Vic, top Tas, to the SA border; *O.w. olivia* in top of NT and WA; and *O.w. hypochlorus* in S SA.

HABITS: Low flying in open woodland. Foodplants are many grasses including *Cynodon, Panicum, Paspalum* and *Imperata* sp.

Pale-orange Darter *Telicota colon*

ID: Very similar to several other darter species, most from E Australia, but only it and *T. augias* can be found in NT. In the east from Cape York to S NSW coastal, and records from one small area in the Pilbara, WA. Small at 28mm wingspan.

HABITS: Flies close to ground in open woodland and grassland. Foodplants include reeds and grasses in the genera *Chrysopogon*, *Sorghum* and *Phragmites*.

Bright-orange Darter *Telicota augias*

ID: One of several similar *Telicota* sp. Found in Cape York and
tropical Qld coast, N NT and the Kimberleys, WA. Wingspan 28mm.

HABITS: Occurs in and near rainforests which host its single
foodplant, *Flagellaria indica*.

Orange Palm Dart *Cephrenes augiades*

ID: Large species, wingspan 37–41mm, with very dark brown wings with cream patterns. Includes a fully dark form with no upperside markings. Native along E coast from Cape York, Qld, to Vic border, and introduced to discrete areas in WA, NT and Melbourne gardens.

HABITS: Originally mainly a rainforest species, now also in gardens with palms. Flies 2m or more above understorey. Foodplants include many palms, including in genera *Calamus*, *Livistonia*, *Licuala* and *Carpentaria*.

Orange Swift *Sabera dobboe*

ID: Deep reddish-brown, medium sized, wingspan 30mm.
Found along Qld coast from Cape York to about Rockhampton.

HABITS: Flies mainly in rainforests and nearby clearings.
Foodplants mainly palm lilies in the genus *Cordyline*.

SWALLOWTAILS –
FAMILY PAPILIONIDAE

Mostly large and showy butterflies. There are 18 Australian swallowtail species out of 550 species worldwide. As the wings are not joined in flight (as they are in moths) their flight can seem erratic, though strong. Some have 'tails' at the tips of the hindwings. At rest the wings are usually held upright and closed, although when in cold pre-flight stage they can be partly open, or rarely fully open.

The eggs, laid singly on leaves, are smooth spheres (other families can have ribbed and sculpted eggs). Caterpillars are squat and usually fatter at the head end. Just behind the head they have an organ called the osmoterium, which is hidden, and only everted as a startle response. It looks like a letter Y or a bit like a snake tongue, and some caterpillars have false eyespots at the front of the body to offer a further element of surprise for potential predators. To add to the display, a strong smell is emitted, which can repel some predators like ants.

Ulysses Swallowtail caterpillar with extended osmoterium.

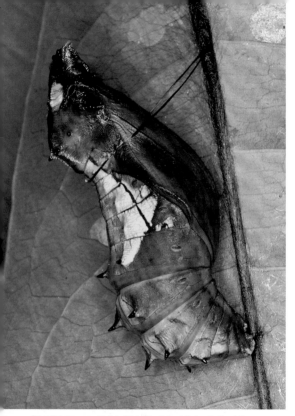

Cairns Birdwing pupa, with its 'safety belt', called a girdle, keeping it upright.

Macleay's Swallowtail *Graphium macleayanum*

ID: Member of the 'triangle' genus, with both sexes possessing small tails at tips of hindwings. Two subspecies: *G.m. maclayanum* from N Qld to the Vic border; and *G.m. moggana* in E Vic and W Tas. Wingspan 55mm.

HABITS: Flies high up and is territorial, with males hilltopping. Found in rainforest and other wet forests such as the beech forests of Tas. Foodplants include, among others, camphor laurel trees and brush wilga (*Geijera salicifolia*) in the north and *Antherosperma moschatum* in the south.

Typical frantic feeding pose for Macleay's Swallowtail, which never seems to settle down.

Blue Triangle *Graphium choredon*

ID: One of the more common and better-known swallowtails, with sky blue markings against a black background. Found from Cape York, Qld, to the Vic border. Wingspan 60mm.

HABITS: Adults fly fast and erratically, often very high up in rainforest and other moist forest canopies. Often seen at flowers, but never in a relaxed sitting pose. Many foodplants, including *Endiandra*, dogwoods in the genera *Beilschmiedia* and *Litsea*, the weed camphor laurel tree *Cinnamomum camphora,* and other laurel species.

Pale Blue Triangle *Graphium eurypylus*

ID: Similar to Blue Triangle but much paler and with main patches of colour on upperwings breaking up into small patches on edges. Two subspecies on mainland: *G.e. lycaon* from Cape York, Qld, through to N NSW and intermittently further south; and *G.e. nyctimus* in NW NT. Wingspan 60mm.

HABITS: Flies high in rainforests and nearby wet forests, and sometimes gardens. Foodplants include trees and shrubs in the genera *Desmos*, *Uvaria* and *Artabotrys*, and introduced custard apples (*Annona muricata*) in gardens.

Female of the east-coast subspecies *G.e. lycaon*.

55

Green-spotted Triangle *Graphium agamemnon*

ID: Bright green spots on black wings make for easy ID. Also differs from the similar Green Triangle, *G.macfarlanei*, by having small tails on hindwings. Found in coastal Qld from Cape York to about Rockhampton. Wingspan 65mm.

HABITS: A very fast and erratic flyer. Never settles down once in the warm sun. Flies very high in rainforest canopies and comes down to feed on flowers on forest edges. Big variety of foodplants, including soursop and custard apple, *Annona muricata*, and *Cyathostemma*, *Goniothalamus* and *Polyalthia* sp.

Red-bodied Swallowtail *Pachliopta polydorus*

ID: Large swallowtail with elongate rather than round hindwings, with six prominent red spots along the underside of hindwings. Found along tropical N Qld coast to Cape York and Torres Strait. Wingspan 75mm.

HABITS: Found in rainforests and monsoon forests. Foodplants include the *Aristolochia* and *Pararistolochia* vines, which it shares with the birdwing butterflies.

Orchard Swallowtail *Papilio aegeus*

ID: Large dark butterfly. Similar to *P. fuscus* but lacks the tails on hindwings and has a wingspan of about 105mm. Common from Cape York and E Qld, down to Vic and around Darwin, NT.

HABITS: Fast bobbing flight. Found in wet and dry forests and in gardens and citrus plantations. Main foodplants are *Citrus* sp, and many related native plants such as *Boronia and Flindersia.*

Male.

Female.

Capaneus Swallowtail and
Canopus Swallowtail *Papilio fuscus*

ID: Large, almost black with white markings. Both sexes have
tails on the hindwings. Wingspan 85–90mm. Three subspecies:
P.f. capaneus (Capaneus Swallowtail) along the entire Qld coast;
P.f. canopus (Canopus Swallowtail) in N NT and the Kimberleys, WA;
and *P.f. indicatus* in the Torres Strait.

HABITS: Found in open woodlands and rainforest, and gardens.
Main foodplants are in the Rutaceae Family, including *Citrus*,
Glycosmis and *Clausena* sp.

Capaneus Swallowtail.

Dingy Swallowtail *Papilio anactus*

ID: This is a small orchard butterfly, different by size, wingspan only 70mm, and forewings with bold off white markings. Found from Cairns, Qld, through to most of E NSW and Vic to Adelaide SA.

HABITS: Found in open woodlands and in gardens. Males hilltop and defend territories. Foodplants mostly *Citrus* sp.

Ulysses Swallowtail *Papilio ulysses*

ID: Nothing else like this symbol of N Qld. Occurs patchily from Cape York down to Sarina. Wingspan 105mm.

HABITS: Flies very high, mainly in rainforests, only rarely coming down to feed at lower flowers, although can sometimes be attracted to bright blue objects. Foodplants are mainly species of *Meliope* and *Flindersia*.

Chequered Swallowtail *Papilio demoleus*

ID: The bold cream markings and lack of hindwing tails separate this species from any similar butterflies. Wingspan about 75mm. Migratory and found seasonally over most of Australia.

HABITS: Fast flyer. One of the species where the males will use sandy margins of water to drink. Foodplants are species of *Cullen* (Fabaceae) and *Citrus*.

Big Greasy *Cressida cressida*

ID: Both sexes have semi-transparent upperwing, and female has a smoky or 'greasy' look. Found from Cape York, Qld, to N NSW and in N NT. Wingspan 70–80mm.

HABITS: Slow flyer, mainly in open woodland. Foodplants are *Aristolochia* sp and *Pararistolochia* vines (same as the birdwing).

Late-stage caterpillar.

Male.

Cairns Birdwing *Ornithoptera euphorion*

ID: Unmistakable. Very large. Upperwings green and black in male, mostly black with yellow and white markings in female. Found from about Cooktown to Mackay, Qld. A smaller species, Richmond Birdwing (*O. richmondia*), occurs in the NSW/Qld Border Ranges and Sunshine Coast hinterland. Wingspan 125–150mm.

HABITS: Flies high in rainforests. Foodplants are species of the *Aristolochia* and *Pararistolochia* vines.

Male.

Last-stage caterpillar.

Female.

WHITES AND YELLOWS – FAMILY PIERIDAE

Australia has 35 species out of 1,100 worldwide. Medium-sized butterflies, the upperwings are commonly white or yellow, with more important diagnostic features often found on the underside. The eggs are elongate like little barrels, also usually yellow, and laid in numbers on leaves. Caterpillars are covered in short, usually white hairs, and the pupa is generally attached to the plants. Average wingspans are 40–50mm.

Caterpillars of the Union Jack, *Delias mysis*, on mistletoe.

Lemon Migrant *Catopsilia pomona*

ID: Pure yellow, or as a paler whitish form with a thin brown
outline. The 'migrants' in this genus have a variable range,
breeding in the tropics but coming south in the warmer months.
Ranges across northern Australia down to Esperance in WA, Alice
in NT and S NSW.
Wingspan 58mm.

HABITS: Flies high
and fast when
migrating, but
does feed on low
flowers along the
way. Foodplants are
species of *Cassia* and
Senna.

Variant from the east.

Variant from WA.

Orange Migrant *Catopsilia scylla*

ID: Most of the time upperside has white forewings and deep yellow hindwings. The range of this migrating butterfly is from the Kimberleys, WA, through the top half of NT and Qld, and along the E coast to S NSW. Wingspan 54mm.

HABITS: Flies very fast when migrating, settling to feed on lower flowers. Seen mainly in summer, with winter range not yet known. Foodplants are species of *Senna*.

Common Grass Yellow *Eurema hecabe*

ID: The grass yellows are seven species of small almost pure yellow butterflies, with wingspans around 30–35mm; this is the largest at 40mm. It is found across the tropics of WA, NT and Qld and can migrate down to S NSW in the summer.

HABITS: Flies low in open woodlands and grasslands. Broad range of foodplants including *Cassia*, *Senna*, *Acacia* and *Trifolium* sp.

Australian Gull *Cepora perimale*

ID: A white butterfly with a black border with white 'spots'. Similar to others, but the two main spots on the upper hindwings, and the yellow to brown underside, are diagnostic. Found in N WA and NT, and in the E from Cape York, Qld, to halfway down NSW, with occasional sightings in Vic. Wingspan 43mm.

HABITS: Fast flyer in many habitats from rainforest to open grassy woodlands. Foodplants are species of caper shrubs, genus *Capparis*.

Common Albatross *Appias paulina*

ID: Upperside a little like Cabbage White, with two black spots on forewing of male, but larger with faster flight and underside has largely yellow hindwings. Found along entire Qld coast and seasonally along the entire NSW and E Vic coast and NE Tas. Wingspan 53mm.

HABITS: Found in rainforests and sometimes in open woodlands. Foodplant is mainly the white myrtle, *Drypetes deplanchei*, and caper shrubs, *Capparis* sp.

Grey Albatross *Appias melania*

ID: Both the upperside and underside hindwings are grey. Found along tropical N Qld coast, though sometimes migrates to an area in central Qld coast. Wingspan 55mm.

HABITS: Found in the tableland rainforests. Foodplant is the white myrtle, *Drypetes* sp.

Male.

Female.

Pearl whites *Elodina* sp.

ID: The seven species of pearl whites are very hard to distinguish, especially in the field. They have a combination of white/pale grey uppersides, and sometimes some yellow on the underside hindwing. Most are found along Qld to N NSW coastal areas. However, if you spot one in NT it will either be Small Pearl White, *Elodina walkeri*, with white upperside, or the migratory Narrow-winged Pearl White, *Elodina padusa*, with a hint of yellow on the upperwings. Wingspans 35–40mm.

HABITS: Flies in rainforests and monsoon forests. Foodplant is the wild caper, *Capparis sepiaria*.

Glistening Pearl White, *Elodina queenslandica*.

Spotted Jezebel *Delias aganippe*

ID: The jezebels have bold red markings on the underside hindwings.
Spotted Jezebel stands out by having red egg shapes against
a black wing border. Found from S Qld coast through most of
NSW and Vic, to eastern SA, and on the SW coastal strip in WA.
Wingspan 60mm.

HABITS: Flies in open woodlands, often with a gliding style.
Foodplants are mistletoes (*Amyema* sp) and sandalwoods
(*Santalum* sp).

Common Jezebel *Delias nigrina*

ID: Distinctive markings as in the picture, similar to Imperial Jezebel, but the red markings are much thinner. Found from Cape York, Qld, down to Vic border. Wingspan 55mm.

HABITS: Flies high but does come down to lower flowers. Found in upland and lowland rainforests and open woodlands. Foodplants are many species of mistletoe in *Amyema* and *Dendrophthoe* genera.

Imperial Jezebel *Delias harpalyce*

ID: Similar to Common Jezebel, but larger and with red underwing markings much broader. Found in E NSW, even inland over the ranges, and most of Vic. Wingspan 70mm.

HABITS: Flies high in the canopy of various types of woodlands which have mistletoes on which they breed. Foodplants *Amyema*, *Dendrophthoe* and *Mullerina* sp.

Northern Jezebel *Delias argenthona*

ID: Rather than a red stripe or red circles or ellipses, as with other jezebels, it has elongate red lozenge shapes on the underside hindwings. Found along all of Qld coast and eastern inland, and E NSW to the Vic border. Wingspan 60mm.

HABITS: Flies high among inland dry woodland to coastal paperbark woodland. Foodplants are mistletoes, including *Diplatia*, *Muellerina*, *Dendrophthoe* and *Santalum* sp.

Union Jack *Delias mysis*

ID: Similar to other jezebels from above, but underside wing pattern has distinctive red band and is mainly white and yellow, rather than black and grey. Found along Qld coast from Cape York to about Mackay and sometimes around Sunshine Coast. A very rare subspecies, *D.m. onca*, found in top of NT and Broome, WA.

HABITS: Flies high in mangroves, tea tree swamps and rainforests. Foodplants are *Dendrophthoe* mistletoes.

Caper White *Belenois java*

ID: Similar to other whites from above, but underside hindwing pattern of yellow 'spots' is diagnostic. A migratory species, seasonally found over most of the warmer parts of the mainland, and sometimes in Tas, but not in the SW of WA. Wingspan 55mm.

HABITS: Often on the move, flying all day and resting at night, through most inland habitats. Foodplants are mainly caper shrubs, *Capparis* sp, and the Warrior Bush, *Apophyllum* sp, in the south.

Caper White drinking from the mud of a creek edge.

Black-spotted White *Leptosia nina*

ID: Off-white wings, with a little black just on the outer edge, and one spot on the upperside forewings. Found in the Kimberleys, WA.

HABITS: Flies low in monsoon forests and along watercourses. Foodplants are caper bushes, *Capparis* sp.

Cabbage White *Pieris rapae*

ID: Often the most commonly seen butterfly in human habitats. Introduced to veggie gardens in most parts of the world. White with two black spots on upperside forewing, and one spot on hindwing.

HABITS: Found mainly in gardens and on farms, as their foodplants do not normally grow in native habitats. With up to five generations a year, this is a constant pest of many leafy vegetable crops.

NYMPHS AND BROWNS – FAMILY NYMPHALIDAE

The nymphs are 81 Australian species, out of 6,000 worldwide, of medium-sized, mostly brown patterned butterflies. Typical rest position is with wings upright, closed, showing the underside. This can be very cryptic among dry vegetation, especially as many species prefer shade to sunlit habitats. Bolder patterns, including eyespots, are sometimes on the upperside wings, which can be used to startle a predator when flicking the wings open. The subfamily Danainae contains the larger and more showy species, with the famous Wanderer butterfly among them.

Both eggs and caterpillars have several shapes, and caterpillars sometimes have bold striped warning colours. The pupae are smooth, lozenge shaped, and usually hang upside-down on the foodplant.

Pupa of Common Crow, *Euploea corinna*.

Evening Brown *Melanitis leda*

ID: Medium-sized brown identified by the pattern of eyespots on underwings and a twin white spot on the upperside forewings. Found along all of E Qld, N NSW coastal, and N NT. Wingspan 60mm.

HABITS: As the name suggests, flies in the evenings, and early mornings. Found in many habitats from rainforest to open woodland and gardens. Foodplants are a variety of natives such as *Heteropogon* and *Imperata*, and non-natives like *Sorghum* and *Melinis* sp.

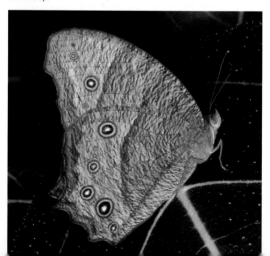

Orange Bush-brown
Mycalesis [Mydosama] terminus

ID: Small brown with a bold series of eyespots along the underwings. Found along entire Qld coastal zone. Wingspan 40mm.

HABITS: Flies in shady habitats in and on the edges of forests, and uses rotting fruit as well as flowers for food. Foodplants include *Imperata*, *Themeda* and *Panicum* sp.

Common Ringlet *Hypocysta metirius*

ID: Very small for a brown. Pattern of spots is similar in other species in this genus, but distinct at fine detail level. Found in patches from N Qld coast through all of E NSW to Vic border. Wingspan 30mm.

HABITS: Males are territorial and hilltop in open patches, otherwise in and on the edges of forests. Foodplants are grasses such as *Cynodon* and *Eriachne* sp.

Northern Ringlet *Hypocysta irius*

ID Very similar to the Common Ringlet, but with the two eyespot patterns on the underside hindwings darker and bolder on a more orange background, and upperside forewings with orange surrounded by brown. Found along entire Qld coast and far N NSW coast. Wingspan 34mm.

HABITS: Found in moist forests from rainforests to shady Eucalypt forests. Foodplants not well known, but basically grasses, family Poaceae.

Orange Ringlet *Hypocysta adiante*

ID: Very bright orange version of similar patterned species in this genus. Two subspecies: *H.a. adiante* along all Qld and NSW coast; and *H.a. antirius* in N NT. Wingspan 30mm.

HABITS: Flies in open woodlands and grasslands. Foodplants are grasses, especially in the genus *Themeda*.

The NT subspecies *H.a. antirius*.

Swordgrass Brown *Tisiphone aboena*

ID: Six subspecies in many shades of brown. In general a very dark butterfly with two very bold eyespots on the underside hindwings, and a spot on the underside forewing which has a blue centre. Found from Sunshine Coast, Qld, south to Vic, in subspecies patches. Wingspan about 55mm.

HABITS: Fly in many types of forest and heath. Males hilltop. Foodplants are many sedges of the genus *Gahnia*.

Opposite: *T.a. aboena.*

Helena Brown *Tisiphone helena*

ID: Similar to other *Tisiphone* species, but underwings very much paler, and both sides have more bright yellow. Found along N Qld Tableland and less so along the tropical coast. Wingspan 46–55mm.

HABITS: Flies in rainforests and wet sclerophyll forests in uplands up to 1,200m. Foodplant is the Red-fruit Saw-sedge, *Gahnia sieberiana*, and other *Gahnia* sp.

Silver Xenica *Oreixenica lathoniella*

ID: Bold geometric patterns, especially on underside hindwing, along with two strong eyespots. Four subspecies: *O.l. herceus* in NSW and Vic, and *O.l. barnardi*, *O.l. lathoniella* and *O.l. laranda* all in Tas. Wingspan about 30mm.

HABITS: Found in open forests, especially in subalpine areas. Some roost communally in swamps. Foodplants are grasses of *Poa* and *Microlaena* sp.

O.l. herceus subspecies in NSW.

Tasmanian Alpine Xenica *Oreixenica ptunarra*

ID: Very similar to the Silver Xenica, but differs in the markings on the underside hindwing being cream on brown, rather than bright white/silver on brown. Found in inland Tas only. Wingspan 28mm.

HABITS: Flies in open woodlands and grass plains away from coast, often around swamps and other water bodies. Foodplants are grasses of the genus *Poa*.

Striped Xenica *Oreixenica kershawi*

ID: Similar to the Silver and Tasmanian Alpine Xenicas, but silver markings form narrow bands on underside, and with smaller eyespots. Three subspecies: *O.k. kershawi* in SE NSW and NE Vic; *O.k. ella* in one tiny area in N NSW Great Dividing Range; and *O.k. kanunda* on the S Vic/SA border. Wingspan 34mm.

HABITS: Flies low to the ground in open woodland clearings, and subalpine woodlands and grasslands up to 1,300m. Foodplants are grasses in the *Poa* and *Tetrarrhena* genera.

Klug's Xenica *Geitoneura klugii*

ID: Among its busy patterns there is only one eyespot per upperside and underside forewing. Found in E NSW, most of Vic, S SA and S WA. Wingspan 40mm.

HABITS: Flies very low and settles on bare ground. Found from open woodlands to semi-arid shrubland. Foodplants include grasses such as *Joycea* and *Poa* sp.

Klug's Xenica in Tasmania.

Hobart Brown *Argynnina hobartia*

ID: In Tasmania only, with three closely spaced eyespots on upperside forewings. Three subspecies: *A.h. hobartia* in E; *A.h. tasmanica* in W; and *A.h. montana* in high mountains. Wingspan 30–33mm.

HABITS: Flies mainly low in the sun and perches with wings open. Found from open woodland to montane heath, up to about 1,000m. Foodplants are grasses including *Poa* sp.

Common Brown *Heteronympha merope*

ID: Three subspecies: *H.m. merope* from SE Qld through NSW and
Vic to Adelaide, SA; *H.m. duboulayi* in SW WA; and *H.m. salazar* in
Tas. Wingspan about 70mm.

HABITS: Broad habitat use from open woodlands to grasslands,
and up to 1,250m altitude. Females can spend summers inactive in
groups, and so have long lives. Foodplants are mainly grasses such
as *Poa* and *Cynodon* sp.

Opposite: *H.m. duboulayi* from WA.

H.m. merope from ACT.

Bright-eyed Brown *Heteronympha cordace*

ID: Dark brown upperwing, paler underwing. Boldly patterned with eyespots on both wings above and below. Five subspecies found in patches along E NSW, most of Vic, and two in Tas (one pictured here). Wingspan 38–42mm.

HABITS: Found in swamps and along creeklines in high country, up to 1,800m altitude in NSW and 1,000m in Tas. Foodplants are sedges in the *Carex* genus.

Banks's Brown *Heteronympha banksii*

ID: Similar to Spotted Brown (*H. paradelpha*), differs by underside hindwings more grey-orange than bright orange. Three subspecies: *H.b. banksii* along most of NSW and E Vic Great Dividing Range; *H.b. mariposa* in the Bunya Mtns and D'Aguilar Range: and *H.b. nevina* in a tiny range in W Vic. Wingspan 48mm.

HABITS: Found in open forests and rainforests up to about 900m altitude. Foodplants are grasses of *Poa*, *Carex* and *Ghania* sp.

H.b. banksii female.

Shouldered Brown *Heteronympha penelope*

ID: Similar to Common Brown, but underside hindwings with only very subtle markings on pale brown background. Female similar to male, unlike Common Brown, in which female has large plain orange areas. Four subspecies: *H.p. penelope* along E NSW and Vic and into Tas; *H.p. alope* in SW Vic and SE corner SA; *H.p. diemeni* and *H.p. panope* in Tas. Wingspan 55mm.

HABITS: Flies low in open grassy woodlands. Found up to 1,600m on the mainland and 1,200m in Tas. Foodplants are grasses in the *Poa*, *Austrodanthonia* and *Themeda* genera.

H.p. penelope in Tasmania.

Leprea Brown *Nesoxenica leprea*

ID: Very bold patches of yellow across dark black/grey upperwings. Found only in Tas with two subspecies: *N.l. leprea* and *N.l. elia*. Wingspan 31mm.

HABITS: Found in beech forests and even pencil pine forests at up to 1,200m altitude. Foodplant is a sedge, *Uncinia tenella*.

Tailed Emperor *Charaxes sempronius*

ID: No similar species. Found through E Qld, E NSW, and separately in N NT and the Kimberleys, WA. Wingspan 90mm.

HABITS: Found in many open habitats, including gardens. Males hilltop. Very wide selection of foodplants including sp of *Acacia*, *Brachychiton*, *Cassia*, *Albizia*, *Celtis* and more.

Newly emerged adults.

Early-stage caterpillar

White Nymph *Mynes [Symbrenthia] geoffroyi*

ID: Upperwings dull white with black border. Underside dark grey with yellow edges and single red spots on forewing and hindwing. Found along most of Qld coast to NSW Border Ranges. Wingspan 60mm.

HABITS: Rainforests up to about 800m. Foodplants include stinging nettles in the genus *Dendrocnide*, and native mulberries in the genus *Pipturus*.

Australian Fritillary *Argynnis [Argyreus] hyperbius*

ID: Unmistakable orange butterfly with black spots. Has a very restricted range and is rarely seen. Found in swamps in the Qld/NSW border area. Sightings need to be recorded via butterfly societies or directly in iNaturalist. Wingspan 60–65mm.

HABITS: Lives in freshwater swamps, and sedge-lands. Food plant is a tiny violet, *Viola betonicifolia*, which is restricted to these wetlands.

A similar form from Asia, which is almost identical to the Australian one.

Red Lacewing *Cethosia cydippe*

ID: Bold red, white and black on the upperwings form unmistakable
pattern. Found from Cape York to about Townsville, Qld. Wingspan
about 75mm.

HABITS: Flies in and on the edges of rainforests and riverine forests.
Often perches with wings open. Main foodplant is the vine *Adenia
heterophylla*.

Male.

Orange Lacewing *Cethosia penthesilea*

ID: Smaller and more orange than Red Lacewing. Ranges do not overlap – Orange Lacewing found only in the top of NT. Wingspan 66mm. Active Apr–Jul.

HABITS: Flies in rainforest and monsoon vine forests. Foodplant is a vine *Adenia heterophylla*.

Cruiser *Vindula arsinoe*

ID: Very bold orange colour stands out. Differs from similar but rarely seen Orange Emperor by lack of small tails on hindwings. Found in patches from Cape York to about Rockhampton, Qld. Wingspan about 85mm.

HABITS: Flies in sunny patches in rainforests and riverine scrub, where males often perch with open wings, but females spend more time higher up. Foodplants include the vine *Adenia heterophylla* and *Passiflora* sp.

Male.

Female.

Leopard *Phalanta phalantha*

ID: Similar to Cruiser, but much smaller and lacks the single small eyespots on upper hindwings. Found only in NW NT. Wingspan 45mm.

HABITS: Flies in coastal woodlands and monsoon forests. Foodplants are the red-fruited large shrubs of the genus *Flacourtia*.

Common Eggfly *Hypolimnas bolina*

ID: Female variable, male with four bold spots on very dark blue wings. Normally found from Cape York, Qld, to N NSW coastal, and N NT and WA, but seasonally can be throughout Qld, NSW, Vic and E Tas. Wingspan 75–85mm.

HABITS: Low flying and territorial. Many habitats, but usually close to creeks and gullies. Many foodplants including the weed *Synedrella nodiflora* and *Asystasia* and *Dipteracanthus* sp.

Male (left) and female in courtship.

Female, Qld.

Blue-banded Eggfly *Hypolimnas alimena*

ID: Sky blue borders of wings, especially in male. Found along entire Qld coast, and a subspecies, *H.a. darwiniensis*, in NW NT. Wingspan about 68mm.

HABITS: Male territorial and often displays upperwings. Found in and near rainforest and riverine scrub. Food plants include *Pseuderanthemum variabilis* and *Asystasia* sp.

Male.

125

Leafwing *Doleschallia bisaltide*

ID: Underwings mimic dead leaf for excellent camouflage, and bold upperside pattern is also diagnostic. Found along entire Qld coast and far N NSW. Wingspan 65mm.

HABITS: Flies fast, flashing orange upperwings when in motion, but disappears when landing with wings closed. Mainly in rainforests. Foodplants include *Pseuderanthemum bicolor, and Asystasia* and *Graptophyllum* sp in gardens.

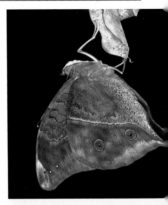

Lurchers *Yoma* sp.

ID: Iron Range Lurcher, *Y. algina*, only recently separated from very similar Australian Lurcher, *Y. sabina*. Both share feature of bold dark yellow stripe across upperwings with Australian Rustic, *Cupha prosope*, but lurchers have wingspan of 70mm compared to 60mm. Lurchers also have cryptic dead-leaf patterns on underwings. *Y. algina* only in Iron Range, *Y. sabina* more widespread in coastal N Qld and N NT.

HABITS: Wet forests and near creeks and swamps. Often perches with wings open. Foodplants are *Dipteracanthus bracteatus* and *Ruellia* sp.

Female Iron Range Lurcher.

Brown Soldier *Junonia hedonia*

ID: Dark brown with a sequence of eyespots along both hindwing and forewing undersides. Found along entire Qld coast and across NT to far NE WA. Wingspan 50mm.

HABITS: Fast flyer, keeping wings closed and cryptic when settled. Found in paperbark and other coastal swamps. Foodplants include the swamp-weed *Hygrophila* and the 'wild petunia' *Ruellia tuberosa*.

Blue Argus *Junonia orithya*

ID: Small distinctive butterfly with upperside hindwings deep blue, especially in male. Found in E Qld, N NT and NE WA. Wingspan 40mm.

HABITS: Flies in open woodland, sometimes settling on ground with wings open. Many foodplants including *Brunoniella*, *Justicia* and *Thunbergia* sp.

Meadow Argus *Junonia villida*

ID: One of the most common butterflies in Australia, found in all states. Prominent eyespot combination and small size are diagnostic. Wingspan 45mm.

HABITS: Flies close to ground and often settles with open wings. Open woodland, grassland and coastal vegetation. Many foodplants including plantains in the genus *Plantago*, and *Ruellia*, *Goodenia* and *Lantana* sp.

Australian Painted Lady *Vanessa kershawi*

ID: Common and widespread. Pattern of black and orange is distinctive, only confused with the introduced European Painted Lady, *V. cardui*, which is now established, though rarely seen, around Perth. Found over most of Qld, NSW, Vic, Tas, SA and E and S WA. Wingspan 58mm.

HABITS: Many habitats, from open woodland to grassland and gardens. Settles with wings partly open. Foodplants include *Bractaentha*, *Rodanthe* and *Ammobium* sp.

Male.

Late-stage caterpillar.

Australian Admiral *Vanessa itea*

ID: Very bold pattern of yellow patches on almost black upper forewings is diagnostic. Found from S Qld through most of NSW, Vic, Tas and to Adelaide SA. Also patches near Alice Springs, NT, and near Perth, WA.

HABITS: Along creeks and in open woodland and gardens. Males do hilltop displays with open wings. Foodplants include nettles in genus *Urtica*, and *Pipturis* and *Parietaria* sp.

Hamadryad *Tellervo zoilus*

ID: Small, elongate-winged, black and white butterfly with distinctive patterns. Found in N Qld, with a different subspecies, *T.z. gelo*, in Cape York. Wingspan 40mm.

HABITS: Flies in rainforest. Males sometimes use sunny patches to display. Foodplants are vines in the genus *Parsonsia*.

Common Crow *Euploea corinna [core]*

ID: There are nine species of crow butterflies with similar black with white wing markings, therefore species ID is best done with pictures of all to compare. The Common Crow is found from the Kimberleys, WA, along N NT and through much of Qld, with some movement to NSW and Vic. Wingspan 75mm.

HABITS: Slow flyer through many shady forests and watercourse habitats. Long lived as they group and cease activity during dry seasons/winters. Broad variety of foodplants including *Ficus* sp, *Nerium* sp of oleander, and *Hoya* sp.

Late-stage caterpillar.

Lesser Wanderer *Danaus petilia [chrysippus]*

ID: Common. Similar to Orange Tiger, which is only found in N NT. Occurs all over Australia, although only seasonally in Vic and Tas. Wingspan 60mm.

HABITS: Found in open habitats, including the dry interior. Many foodplants utilised, including *Brachystelma*, *Marsdenia*, *Calotropis* and *Asclepias* sp.

Wanderer *Danaus plexippus*

ID: Large famous butterfly, introduced to Australia and now
established along most of Qld coast, and seasonally into E NSW, all
Vic, SE SA, and around Perth WA. Wingspan 90mm.

HABITS: Slow flying, often gliding, in a wide variety of habitats,
including in gardens. Foodplants include the milkweed in the genus
Asclepias, and *Calotropis* and *Stapelia* sp.

Black-and-white Tiger *Danaus affinis*

ID: Shape of white patterns on near-black upperwings are diagnostic. Found along entire Qld coast, N NSW coast, in N NT and just into N WA. Wingspan 64mm.

HABITS: Found in coastal swamps, including brackish and mangrove swamps. Foodplant is a vine, *Cynanchum carnosum*.

Blue Tiger *Tirumala hamata*

ID: Large butterfly with an unmistakable pattern of complex blue markings against black. Found along entire Qld coast, NW NT, and seasonally in NSW and N Vic. Wingspan 75mm.

HABITS: Long lived, slow flyer, found in rainforests and monsoon forests. Undertakes massive migrations, which result in large aggregations along creeks in coastal N Qld during the dry season. Foodplants are vines including *Secamone*, *Marsdenia* and *Cynanchum* sp.

Glasswing *Acraea andromacha*

ID: Black and white patterns on almost see-through wings. Only similar to Big Greasy, but smaller and lacks bold red spots on wing margins. Found in E Qld, E NSW and sometimes into Vic, also in N NT and N and W WA. Wingspan 55mm.

HABITS: Flies and glides low in open woodlands and grasslands. Foodplants include passionfruits, *Passiflora* sp, and spade flowers, *Hybanthus* sp.

Tawny Coster *Acraea terpsicore*

ID: This species is not yet in most Australian butterfly books as it has only very recently been accidentally introduced into the top of NT, WA and Qld. Originating from southern Africa, it is now quite established. Wingspan about 60mm.

HABITS: Presently found in open grassland feeding on a variety of flowers.

METALMARKS –
FAMILY RIODINIDAE

The 'Metalmarks' name comes from fine metallic colour flecks on many species' wings. This family has about 1,500 species of often stunningly beautiful butterflies worldwide. Papua New Guinea has many species, but in Australia only one exists, which is very much like the nymphs in general appearance.

Both the caterpillar and pupa are spiky/hairy, and the purple egg is a very distinctive barrel shape. Some older books include the Riodinidae as a subfamily of the Lycaenidae, the Blues, but today it is generally considered to warrant status as a family in its own right.

Harlequin Metalmark *Praetaxila segecia*

ID: Prominent white band across both upperside and underside of the forewings. The body and legs have a strong yellow colour. Found at the tip of Cape York Peninsula, Qld. Wingspan 45mm.

HABITS: Lives in the rainforest patches of the upper Cape. Foodplant is a rainforest tree, *Rapanea porosa*.

Male.

BLUES – FAMILY LYCAENIDAE

There are 142 Australian species in this family, from a worldwide total of more than 6,000 named species of mainly small butterflies. The blue colours are generally only on the upperwings, and many species have other colours, such as copper and even purple. The underwings tend to be brown, cream or white with fine patterns. Some species have fine tails on the hindwings. At rest most keep the wings closed upright, some partly open, and very rarely fully open. So the bold colours are usually only revealed in flight. Eggs are flattened ovoids, with fine patterns, and the larvae are flattened and tough 'skinned'. Some have special organs on the rear segments which produce sweet secretions as reward for ants which protect those species' caterpillars. Among such species are caterpillars which feed on the ant larvae. Average wingspans 25–35mm.

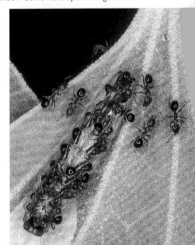

Caterpillar of Macqueen's Imperial Blue, *Jalmenus pseudictinus*, attended by ants of the genus *Froggattella*.

Bright Copper *Paralucia aurifera*

ID: Small butterfly with a coppery coloured large marking on each upperside wing. Found from S Qld coast through E NSW and Vic and into E Tas. Wingspan 25mm.

HABITS: Quick flyer in open forests. Often settles with wings open in sunlight. Foodplants are the mock orange, *Bursaria* sp, and orange thorn, *Pittosporum* sp. Caterpillars attended by ants.

Dull Copper *Paralucia pyrodiscus*

ID: Most similar to the Bright Copper, but differs by its upperside hindwings either not having a distinct copper central marking, or only having a coppery sheen. Found in a NE Qld pocket, then from about Rockhampton south through E NSW and E Vic. Wingspan 26mm.

HABITS: Flies low in open woodlands and often keeping to ridges. Foodplants are shrubs in the genera *Bursaria* and *Pittosporum*. Attended by *Notoncus* sp ants.

Small Copper *Lucia limbaria*

ID: Brown upperside with large copper patches on forewings. Complex patterns on grey underside. Found from about Rockhampton, Qld, south through NSW into Vic, and around Adelaide, SA. Wingspan 25mm.

HABITS: Open grassy habitats. Foodplants are species of the sorrel herb, genus *Oxalis*.

Western Jewel *Hypochrysops halyaetus*

ID: This genus has 18 species in Australia, but only two in WA, where the turquoise colour (compared to a deep blue) distinguishes it from the Fiery Jewel. Found from Perth to about Carnarvon, WA. Wingspan 25mm.

HABITS: Flies fast close to the ground in heath and open sandy woodland habitats. Foodplants are species of *Acacia*, *Jacksonia* and *Daviesia*, on which the caterpillars are attended by ants.

Narcissus Jewel *Hypochrysops narcissus*

ID: As the name suggests, a very showy butterfly. Pure azure and
black upperside, and bold red and gold patterning on underside.
Two subspecies: *H.n. narcissus* along tropical N Qld coast; and
H.n. sabirius in N Cape York. Wingspan 28mm.

HABITS: Found in fresh and brackish swamps, paperbark and
mangrove swamps. Foodplants include mistletoes like *Dendrophthoe*
and *Diplatia* sp, and mangoves such as *Aegiceras*, *Ceriops* and
Rhizophora sp.

Fiery Jewel *Hypochrysops ignitus*

ID: Bright orange markings on underside, and multi-hued blues to coppers at different angles of upperside. Four subspecies: *H.i.ignita* along lower half of Qld coast and all NSW coast; *H.i. erythrina* in patches from Darwin to the Kimberleys; *H.i.chrysonotus* in Far N Qld; and *H.i. olliffi* in patches of SW WA. Wingspan 26mm.

HABITS: Fast flyer through open woodlands and heaths. Males hilltop. Foodplants very numerous, including *Acacia, Alphitonia, Eucalyptus, Prunus* and *Banksia* sp.

Common Oak Blue *Arhopala micale*

ID: Dazzling blue with a black border on upperwings, and small tails on hindwings. Underwings dark brown with blue to red patterns at different angles. Found from Cape York to about Mackay, Qld, and a subspecies in N NT. Wingspan 44mm.

HABITS: Very flashy blue when flying, but disappears when settled with wings closed. Found in many forest types from rainforest and gallery forest to mangroves. Many foodplants, including *Terminalia*, *Hybiscus*, *Buchanania* and *Callophyllum* sp. Caterpillars attended by green tree ants.

Two closed-wing views, showing how shade colours (left) can differ from sun-reflected colours (right).

Satin Azure *Ogyris amaryllis*

ID: Medium-sized blue with very iridescent azure upperwings.
Four subspecies, including a true arid interior one, *O.a. meridionalis*,
found inland in all mainland states. Others along Qld and NSW
coast. Wingspan 35mm.

HABITS: Fast flyer. Settles with closed wings hiding the bright blue.
Found in open woodlands and even mangroves. Foodplants are
mistletoe plants – *Amyema* sp, frequently parasitic on *Casuarina* –
and *Acacia* sp.

Large Bronze Azure *Ogyris idmo*

ID: One of the biggest blues, wingspan 45mm, with upperwings very dark purple/blue. Female with one white patch on forewing. Two subspecies: *O.i. idmo* in patches of SW WA; and *O.i. halmaturia* in a small area on the Vic/SA border.

HABITS: Fast flyer, low through mallee and heath. Associated with *Camponotus* ants.

Common Tit *Hypolycaena phorbas*

ID: Male blue with large single black patch on upperside forewings.
Females replace the black patches with white ones. Hindwings
with two very fine tails. Underside wings white with two spots
on hindwings. Two subspecies: *H.p. phorbas* from Cape York to
Rockhampton, coastal Qld, and *H.p. ingura* in N NT and Kimberleys,
WA. Wingspan 30mm.

HABITS: Found in almost every habitat in the range, as long as the
associated green tree ants, *Oecophylla smaragdina*, are present.
Many foodplants including *Terminallia*, *Syzygnium*, *Senna* and
Cassia sp.

Shining Pencilled Blue
Eirmocides [Candalides] helenita

ID: Striking pure sky blue upperside on male, with pure white undersides on both sexes. Females, pictured here, have no blue. Found along N Qld coast from about Mackay to Cape York. Wingspan 28mm.

HABITS: Flies in rainforests and adjacent woodlands. Foodplants include buttonwood (*Glochidion* sp), laurel tree (*Cryptocarya* sp) and flame tree (*Brachychiton* sp).

Blotched Dusky Blue *Erina [Candalides] acasta*

ID: Tiny. Deep blue/purple upperwing with no pattern. Dark cream underwing. Found from about Bundaberg, coastal Qld, through NSW and Vic to about Adelaide, SA. Also E Tas and separately in SW WA. Wingspan 22mm.

HABITS: Flies low in sandy heath and open woodland. Foodplants are vines in the genus *Cassytha*.

Common Dusky Blue
Erina hyacinthinus [Candalides hyacinthina]

ID: Dark purple-blue upperside with no markings, white underside
with two black spots on edge of forewing. Three subspecies:
C.h. hyacinthinus in patches of Qld coast, E NSW and most of
Vic; *C.h. simplexa* in S SA and patches in S and W WA; *C.h. gilesi*
in small SW corner of WA. Wingspan 28mm.

HABITS: Found from rainforest in Qld to semi-arid woodlands and
heaths in the south. Foodplants are many species of vines in the
genus *Cassytha*.

Copper Pencilled Blue
Cyprotides [Candalides] cyprotus

ID: Upperwings deep blue or brown with dark margins. Underside dark cream. Two subspecies: *C.c. cyprotus* in S Qld and N NSW; *C.c. pallescens* in patches of NSW, Vic-SA border, and SW WA. Wingspan 28mm.

HABITS: Flies in many habitats including open woodland, mallee and heath. Males do hilltopping on exposed rises. Active for only a few weeks in spring. Foodplants include *Grevillea*, *Hakea* and *Jacksonia* sp.

Common Rayed Blue *Candalides heathi*

ID: Very distinctive almost pure white underside with six spots along hindwing margin. Found very patchily in S Qld, E and S NSW, most of Vic and into S SA, and patches in central Australia and parts of WA. Wingspan 28mm.

HABITS: Many habitats from the coast to mallee scrub inland, and subalpine woodlands in the east. Wide variety of foodplants across its range, including *Westringia*, *Plantago*, *Eremophila* and *Stemodia* sp.

Yellow-spot Blue *Candalides xanthospilos*

ID: Very distinctive black/blue upperside with large yellow spot on forewing, and bright white underside. Found along the tropical coast and S Qld, through NSW, and E Vic. Wingspan 25mm.

HABITS: Found in open forests and heath, and partly opens wings when settled. Foodplants are species of riceflower plants, *Pimelea*.

Large Green-banded Blue *Danis danis*

ID: White with sky blue and a black outline on upperside. Bright metallic green patterns on underside. Found from about Cooktown to Townsvillle, Qld, with a subspecies in N Cape York. Wingspan 35mm.

HABITS: Flies slowly in rainforests. Foodplants are vines in the *Connarus*, *Rourea* and *Derris* genera.

Mating pair of Large Green-banded Blues

Small Green-banded Blue *Psychonotis caelius*

ID: Similar to the Large Green-banded Blue, but metallic green stripe along the underside forewings only on the leading edge, not curved over. Found along entire Qld coast and most of NSW coast. Wingspan 30mm.

HABITS: Slow flying in rainforests and other wet shady areas. Foodplants are Sarsparilla, *Alphitonia* sp.

Two-spotted Lineblue *Nacaduba biocellata*

ID: Very small, with upperside purple/blue in male and dark copper in female. Found in every state, including the centre, but missing from N NT and N WA. Wingspan 17mm.

HABITS: Dry open *Acacia* woodlands. Foodplants are *Acacia* flowers. Attended by *Iridomyrmex* and *Technomyrmex* ants.

The more copper-coloured female.   Male.

The closed-wing pose.

Tailed Green-banded Blue *Nacaduba cyanea*

ID: Iridescent green band, can appear blue from some angles, as here. Differs from the other green-banded blues by the forewing underside wing black outline broken into 4 rectangles, and the presence of hindwing tails. Found in Cape York and tropical Qld coast.

HABITS: Found in lowland rainforests. One known foodplant is a vine, *Entada phaseoloides*.

White-banded Lineblue *Nacaduba kurava*

ID: Complex grey/white patterns on underside wings, as pictured here. Upperside wings pure blue in male and black-bordered white/blue in female. Two subspecies: *N.k. parma* along most of Qld coast and into N NSW coast; and *N.k. felsina* in small area of NE NT. Wingspan 24mm.

HABITS: Found in rainforests in Qld and monsoon forests in NT. Foodplants include the vine *Embelia curvinervia* in NT, and *Maesa* sp vines and *Rapanea* sp in Qld.

Speckled Lineblue *Catopyrops florinda*

ID: Small. A dark mauve upperside and very finely patterned dark
cream underside, with a small eyespot on the hindwings. Small
single wing tails. Two subspecies; *C.f. halys* found in S Qld and
coastal NSW, and *C.f. estrella* found in N Qld and patches in N
NT and N WA. Wingspan 22mm. HABITS: Found in rainforests
and riverine scrub. Foodplants include *Caesalpinia*, *Trema* and
Pipturus sp.

Mountain Heath Blue *Neolucia hobartensis*

ID: Tiny, with dark copper upperside and complex speckled underside. Two subspecies, *N.h. hobartensis* in Tas, and along the Great Divide in Vic and S NSW; and *N.h. monticila* on the Great Divide in N NSW. Wingspan 16mm.

HABITS: This is a high-country species occurring from about 300m–1,300m in Tas, and up to 2,190m in NSW. Found in open woodlands and alpine heaths. Foodplants are species of *Epacris*.

Dull Heath Blue *Neolucia mathewi*

ID: Dark copper-brown upperside with no markings. Found in patches along the coast and the Great Dividing Range in NSW, Vic and rarely in Tas. Wingspan 18mm.

HABITS: Flies in coastal heaths and Banksia woodland, and in subalpine heaths. Foodplants and species of the broom heath shrubs *Monotoca* sp.

Fringed Heath Blue *Neolucia agricola*

ID: Very similar to the Mountain Heath Blue, but differs by two pale triangular marks on the hindwing underside. Three subspecies: *N.a.agricola* from S Qld, NSW, Vic to S SA; *N.a. insulana* in Tas, and *N.a. occidens* in S WA (pictured here). Wingspan 20mm.

HABITS: Found in open woodlands and heaths, up to 1,700m in NSW and 1,000m in Tas. Males hilltop. Foodplants are shrubs including *Daviesia*, *Bossiaea*, *Jacksonia* and *Aotus* sp.

Common Imperial Blue *Jalmenus evagoras*

ID: Strong black border around pale blue upperwings. Hindwings with thin black bands and a curly tail. Previously two subspecies, *J.e. evagoras* from S Qld to E Vic, and *J.e. eubulus* in SE Qld – which is now considered a separate species, *Jalmenus eubulus.* Wingspan 35mm.

HABITS: Flies in open woodlands, including brigalow and acacia scrub. Foodplants are various species of *Acacia*. Attended by *Iridomyrmex* ants.

Australian Hairstreak *Pseudalmenus chlorinda*

ID: Very dark brown/black upperside with bold yellow and orange
bands. White underside with thin black and red stripes. Single
tail on hindwings. Variable within those parameters with six
subspecies, three on the mainland in NSW and Vic, and three in Tas.
Wingspan 28mm.

HABITS: Flies and hilltops high in open woodlands and clearings.
Foodplants are species of *Acacia*, with *A. dealbata* and
A. melanoxylon the main ones. Attended by *Anonychomyrma* ants.

P.c. myrsilus from Tasmania.

Saltbush Blue *Theclinesthes serpentatus*

ID: Tiny, deep azure blue upperside and brown/red chequered patterns on the underside. Found from central Qld through most of NSW, S SA, and patches in S NT and W WA. Wingspan 18mm.

HABITS: Flies fast and low, in many open sandy and semi-arid habitats. Foodplants are several genera of saltbush, including *Chenopodium*, *Atriplex* and *Pilostyles* sp. Attended by ants.

Wattle Blue *Theclinesthes miskini*

ID: Very similar to several other *Theclinesthes* species with the two black spots on the hindwing underside. Subtle difference is a more grey-brown underside compared to others. Azure blue with black spots on upperside hindwing edges. Three subspecies, with *T.m. miskini* in most of the mainland, and *T.m. eucalypti* in Cape York. Wingspan 22mm.

HABITS: Flies low in open woodlands, savannah, and semi-arid heath. Males hiiltop. Foodplants are mainly species of *Acacia*, and also some *Eucalyptus, Corymbia* and *Cajanus* sp.

Long-tailed Pea Blue *Lampides boeticus*

ID: Reflective blue upperwings with two eyespots on lower hindwings, and complex cream patterns on underside. Fine tails on hindwings. Found over all of Vic, NSW and most of Qld. Patches in NW NT and Pilbara and SW WA, and sometimes Tas. Wingspan 26mm.

HABITS: Found in various habitats in their broad range, as well as in gardens. Foodplants include many species of pea flowers.

Zebra Blue *Leptotes plinius*

ID: Males with blue upperside and bold brown/cream patterns on the underside, and females with chequered blue patterns on upperside. Found along most of E Qld and NSW with small patches inland, including near Alice, NT. Wingspan 22mm.

HABITS: Found in open woodlands which hold their foodplant, the leadwort *Plumbago zeylanica*, and in gardens with introduced *Plumbago* sp.

Common Grass Blue *Zizina labradus*

ID: Upperside azure blue with no markings, underside pale fawn with subtle marginal bands. Two subspecies: *Z.l. labradus* found all around Australia with a gap in the interior WA deserts, and the Gulf area of Cape York, Qld; *Z.l. labdalon* is at the tip of Cape York. Wingspan 22mm.

HABITS: Found in any grassy habitats in the wild, and in pastures and gardens. Foodplants are legumes like Alfalfa, *Medicago* sp, and beans.

Dainty Grass Blue *Zizula hylax*

ID: Very small with fully blue male and fully dark brown/grey female uppersides. Underside bright cream with speckles. Found along all Qld coast and into N NSW, and near Darwin, NT. Wingspan only 15mm.

HABITS: Slow flyer. Found in paperback swamps, coastal open woodlands and gardens. Foodplants include the fruit rather than leaves of the swampweed *Hygrophila angustifolia*. Also *Dipteracanthus* sp.

Moth Butterfly *Liphyra brassolis*

Brown and orange colours with a broader than normal body. Found along the Qld coast from Cape York to about Mackay, and in NW NT. Wingspan very big for a blues, at 75mm.

HABITS: Not common, but found in many habitats, wherever the green tree ants (*Oecophylla smaragdina*), live. Caterpillars, shaped like an armoured lozenge, live with the ants, and feed on the ant larvae.

GLOSSARY

ANTENNAE: a pair of jointed sensory organs on the head of all insects, mainly used to detect smells. Also known as 'feelers'.

CHRYSALIS: term used for the pupa of mainly butterflies, and some moths

COMPLETE METAMORPHOSIS: growth cycle where the young (larvae) have a different form from the adult, and undergo a pupal stage to become the adult.

EXOSKELETON: tough jointed outer covering, or skeleton, of insects and other arthropods. It is made of chitin and as it does not grow it has to be shed (moulted) periodically to allow the insect to increase in size.

HONEYDEW: a sweet secretion produced by some Lycaenid (Blues) butterflies, which attracts ants. In return the ants protect the caterpillars. Other insect orders, such as hoppers and scale insects (the Hemiptera) also have many honeydew-producing species.

INSTAR: each stage of the growth-cycle of immature insects – the larvae or nymphs. Between each instar the exoskeleton is moulted and replaced with a new larger one to accommodate growth. Butterfly caterpillars have four to five instars.

MOULT: to shed the outer 'skin' or exoskeleton in the process of growth.

PROLEGS: short appendages on the abdomens of most caterpillars, that act like extra legs. The 'normal' longer legs are on the thorax.

PUPA: the usually inactive stage between larvae and adult insects. During this stage the insect undergoes the metamorphosis, or change, of the whole body into the adult form.

SEGMENT: a division of the exoskeleton of all arthropods. Each leg, antenna, and whole body, is divided into segments with a flexible join, allowing the insect to move and flex its body.

TARSI: the last segments of the legs of insects, that act as the 'feet'.

THORAX: the middle of the three main divisions of the insect body, the head-thorax-abdomen sequence. The thorax has three main segments, upon which are mounted the three pairs of legs, and wings if present.

FURTHER READING

BOOKS

*A Field Guide to Butterflies of Australia: Their Life Histories
and Larval Food Plants* by Garry Sankowsky and Geoff Walker.
Reed New Holland. ISBN 978 1 92151 788 4.
All About Butterflies of Australia by Garry Sankowsky.
Reed New Holland. ISBN 978 1 92151 743 3.
Attracting Butterflies to Your Garden by Densey Clyne.
Reed New Holland. ISBN 978 1 87706 984 0.
Butterflies of the World by Adrian Hoskins.
Reed New Holland. ISBN 978 1 92151 733 4.

WEBSITES

Butterflies of Australia – website, run by the Coffs Harbour Butterfly
House: lepidoptera.butterflyhouse.com.au/butter.html
Butterflies Australia – a citizen science project to record butterfly
sightings: butterflies.org.au/external/home
Sustainable Gardening Australia – page about attracting butterflies
to your garden: sgaonline.org.au/butterflies/
iNaturalist – website for recording sightings/distribution of all
organisms: inaturalist.org/

PHOTO CREDITS

All images by Paul Zborowski except for the following:
(a = above, b = below, l = left, r = right)

Alan Daley: page 102

Elizabeth Daley: pages 43a, 104

Kristi Ellingsen: pages 10a, 10b, 11a, 11b, 33a, 147

Simon Grove/TMAG: pages 31, 33b, 34, 38b, 43b, 45, 98, 99, 103,
    105, 110, 111, 131ar, 131b, 132a, 138r, 146, 159a, 172a, 172b,
    175a, 175b, 178b

Kerri-Lee Harris: pages 38a, 39, 40, 80, 88, 141, 163, 174a, 180a, 180b

Fred and Jean Hort: back cover, pages 26, 27, 36b, 37, 42, 64a, 69b,
    72, 77, 106, 123, 128a, 128b, 130, 131al, 136a, 136b, 138a, 150,
    152, 153, 154b, 155, 156, 159b, 161a, 161b, 173a, 173b, 176, 177

Bernhard Jacobi: pages 30a, 30b, 35, 36a, 44, 129, 133a, 169, 178a

Elaine McDonald: pages 108, 112, 113

John Nielsen: pages 23, 29a, 29b, 32b, 53, 55, 61a, 61b, 64b, 73, 79,
    93, 94, 95, 96, 97, 100, 101, 107, 109, 116, 117, 120, 140, 148,
    149, 160, 174b

Peter Samson: pages 144

Garry Sankowsky: pages 22, 24, 74, 75a, 75b, 158

Shutterstock (individual photographer names in brackets): front cover
    (Norbert Orisek); pages 1 (Karen H Black); 19 (Karen Brough);
    25a, 25b, 181a (Peter Waters); 56b (Sharon Haeger); 62 (puyalroyo);
    69a (Moshe Einhorn); 71 (Sourabh Poojary); 81 (Tracey Jones
    Photography); 82, 114a (Ken Griffiths); 83, 179 (Anurag Khese);
    89 (Jude Black); 181b (Jonathan Steinbeck)

Paul Whittington: page 92

INDEX

Reed Concise Guide: Animals of Australia Ken Stepnell
   ISBN 978 1 92151 754 9
Reed Concise Guide: Birds of Australia Ken Stepnell
   ISBN 978 1 92151 753 2
Reed Concise Guide: Frogs of Australia Marion Anstis
   ISBN 978 1 92151 790 7
Reed Concise Guide: Insects of Australia Paul Zborowski
   ISBN 978 1 92554 644 6
Reed Concise Guide: Snakes of Australia Gerry Swan
   ISBN 978 1 92151 789 1
Reed Concise Guide: Spiders of Australia
   Volker W Framenau and Melissa L Thomas
   ISBN 978 1 92554 603 3
Reed Concise Guide: Wild Flowers of Australia Ken Stepnell
   ISBN 978 1 92151 755 6

For details of these books and hundreds of other
Natural History titles see
newhollandpublishers.com
and follow ReedNewHolland on Facebook and Instagram

Our love of butterflies has been reflected in several stamp issues in Australia.